Experiencing
GOD
through
PRAYER

Experiencing
GOD
through
PRAYER

Madame Guyon

𝔀 *Whitaker House*

All Scripture quotations are from the *King James Version* (KJV) of the Bible.

EXPERIENCING GOD THROUGH PRAYER

ISBN: 0-88368-153-6
Printed in the United States of America
Copyright © 1984 by Whitaker House
Cover Photo: H. Armstrong Roberts

Whitaker House
30 Hunt Valley Circle
New Kensington, PA 15068

11 12 13 14 15 16 17 / 08 07 06 05 04 03 02

Contents

Introduction

This little book by Madame Jeanne Guyon is a treasure chest of spiritual wisdom. It contains rich nuggets of truth that could only have been revealed to her by the Spirit of God.

We have for many years seen the name of Jeanne Guyon held in high esteem through the writings of leaders in Christianity such as Andrew Murray, Watchman Nee, Hudson Taylor, and Jesse Penn-Lewis.

Unable to find any of her writings, we began a nationwide search hoping to uncover one of her early manuscripts. When we finally found this book, we immediately knew it must be shared again with Christians in our century.

Madame Guyon was a unique handmaiden of the Lord. Having lived in a degraded society and been imprisoned for her outspoken devotion to God, she wrote commanding and inspiring words urging men and women to turn from the earthly and press on to know God.

While the sentence structure and the language have been revised for today's reader, the profound truths remain untouched.

It is our hope that you will not only experience the presence of God in a fresh and wonderful way, but also that you will desire to share these truths with others.

THE PUBLISHER

Preface

This simple little book was never intended for publication. It was written for a few individuals who had a desire to love God with all their hearts. Because of the great blessing they received in reading the manuscript, they requested additional copies; and this is why I agreed to publish it.

I submit my writings to the judgment of learned and experienced Christians. I do not criticize the divine leadings of others. On the contrary, they only reinforce the teachings I have received.

It is my purpose through the writing of this book to influence the world to love God and to serve Him successfully.

Yet I have written in a simple, easy manner so that even the uneducated and untrained would desire to be truly devoted to God.

If you read without prejudice, you will find hidden in the most common expressions a secret anointing that will cause you to seek the happiness that everyone can and should enjoy.

Perfection is easily obtained when we seek God within ourselves. Some readers may disagree and refer to John 7:34: *"Ye shall seek me, and shall not find me."* However, Matthew 7:7 says, *"Seek, and ye shall find."*

God does not contradict Himself. It is true that he who seeks God, yet is unwilling to forsake his sins, will not find Him. But he who seeks God and forsakes sin will certainly find Him.

Often, because holiness frightens many and answered prayer seems difficult to attain, some are discouraged from taking that first step. But when you understand how easy it is to pray and find joy, you will enjoy praying vigorously. The purpose of this book, then, is to dispel any myths and discuss the advantages of prayer.

If we only knew how much God loves us and wants to communicate with us, we would not set up impossible standards for ourselves. Nor would we become discouraged in obtaining good things from God. After all, it is His earnest intent to give us good things. *"He that spared not his own Son, but delivered him up for us all, how shall he not with him also freely give us all things?"* (Romans 8:32).

We have enough courage and perseverance in our worldly concerns. But in the spiritual realm, there is one thing needed. We must be more like Mary than Martha. Jesus tells us, *"But one thing is needful: and Mary hath chosen that good part, which shall not be taken away from her"* (Luke 10:42). He was referring to the fact that Mary had her priorities centered in knowing and hearing from Jesus. If you are one of those who believe it is not easy to find God, I only ask that you hear my testimony and then try this method for yourself. Your own experience will convince you more than any description I can give you.

Dear reader, study this book with a sincere spirit and a humble mind. If you read to criticize, you will fail to profit from it. It is my desire that as you read it, you will desire to completely devote yourself to God.

God is greatly grieved at the lack of trust among His children. Yet He delights when we come to Him in simple, childlike confidence.

Therefore, for your own salvation, seek only to find the love of God, and you will most assuredly obtain it. The result of following after the Lord will bring you much happiness.

This book was written to instruct you in prayer. It was not meant to offend. Those who seriously desire to know truth will find it.

JEANNE GUYON

One

Thirsting for God

Everyone is capable of praying, but many have the mistaken idea that they are not called to prayer. Just as we are called to salvation, we are called to prayer.

Scripture commands us to *"pray without ceasing"* (1 Thessalonians 5:17). Prayer is nothing more than turning our hearts toward God and receiving His love in turn.

Meditating on God's Word in prayer is desirable, but known by very few. For those who are seeking salvation, meditative prayer is not what God requires of you or what I would recommend.

Are you thirsting for those living waters Jesus promised when He said, *"If any man thirst, let him come unto me and drink"* (John 7:37)?

Are you tired of feeling like a *"broken* [cistern], *that can hold no water"* (Jeremiah 2:13)?

Then come, you starving souls; come and be filled!

Come, bring your affliction, pain, and misery, and you will be comforted!

Come, you who are sick and filled with disease, and you will be healed!

Come, draw near to your Father who desires to embrace you in His loving arms!

Come, you poor, wandering sheep, back to the Shepherd!

Come, sinners, to your Savior!

Come, you who are uneducated in spiritual things! You are not incapable of praying!

Let everyone, without exception, come! For Jesus Christ has called all of you.

Yet those who are without a yielded heart are excused. For there must be a heart yielded before Him to receive His love.

Come, then, give your heart to God and learn the ways of prayer.

For those who have the desire, it is easy to pray. The Holy Spirit has enabled common men to pray great prayers by His gifts and grace.

Prayer can help you to attain perfection, because it will keep you in the presence of God. Genesis 17:1 says, *"Walk before me, and be thou perfect."* We are brought into His presence and kept there without interruption through prayer.

There is only one requirement, though, that you must follow at all times. It will not interfere with outward actions. It may be practiced by princes, kings, priests, soldiers, children, and laborers.

This simple requirement is that you must learn to pray from your heart and not your head.

The reason for this is that man's mind is so limited in its operation, it can only focus on one object at a time. But the prayer offered from the heart cannot be interrupted by reason. Nothing can interrupt this prayer except confused affection. When you have enjoyed God and the sweetness of His love, however, you will find it impossible to set your affections on anything other than Him.

I have found it easy to obtain the presence of God. He desires to be more present to us than we desire to seek Him. He desires to give Himself to us far more readily than we desire to receive Him. We only need to know *how* to seek God, and this is easier and more natural than breathing.

Oh, dear ones, do not think of yourselves as misfits. By prayer you can live in God's presence with as little effort as you live on the very air you are now breathing.

Is it not sinful to neglect prayer? But you do not have to live this way once you have learned this easy method.

Let us prepare our hearts now as we begin our study of prayer.

Two

Scriptural Meditation

There are two ways of introducing you to prayer. One is by meditation on the Word. The other is by reading the Word and then meditating in prayer.

To meditate on God's Word simply means to take a portion of Scripture and begin the following procedure. Read only a small section and allow that passage to be "digested" before going on to another.

Draw from it its fullest meaning. Think it through. Try to relate it to other similar Scriptures. Commit it to memory. Then, having thoroughly examined the passage, proceed to take another one and do the same.

Try not to read more than half a page at a time. It is not the quantity of Scripture you read, but the quality that will be to your benefit.

Those who are fast readers gain no more advantage than a bee would by skimming the surface of a flower rather than penetrating it to extract its pollen.

Speed reading can be used for other subjects, but never for divine truth.

To receive profit from the Word, you must read as I have described. I am certain that by doing this, you will have made meditating on the Word a habit that will cause you to grow as a Christian.

In physical food you receive no nourishment until you chew and swallow the food. The food may taste good in your mouth as you continue to enjoy its flavor. But it is in swallowing and digesting that it benefits the body.

In an act of love, full of respect and confidence in God, swallow the blessed spiritual food He has given to you. It will cause you to become a mature Christian.

May this be a word of caution for beginners: don't wander from truth to truth and from subject to subject.

The right way is to allow each individual truth to be meditated upon while its sweet flavor remains fresh. You certainly would not stuff your mouth with another bite of food until you had swallowed the last one. Scriptural truth should be digested in the same way.

As you form the habit of meditating on God's Word, it will become easier for you to bring to remembrance other Scriptures of the same nature. This will further enhance your ability to bring the Word of God into reality in your life.

The second method is to learn to pray the Word.

When you come to God in prayer, open your Bible to where you have been meditating. Remember at this point that your main objective is to focus on God's presence. Your Scripture verse will keep your mind from straying to other things.

This method of praying can be used by those of you with even a small portion of faith, because it will keep your mind from distractions. This way even a small amount of faith will enlarge in proportion when viewed by itself.

Oh, dear one, God has promised that He would come and make His abode with him who does His will. (See John 14:23.) He has promised to dwell in our innermost beings—the new Holy of Holies.

St. Augustine once blamed himself for all the lost time trying to find God's will when, from the very beginning, he could have done so by this manner of praying the Word.

When you have settled into a peaceful spirit and are fully aware of God's presence; when earthly distractions are not your primary thoughts; when your soul has properly fed on God's Word and you have chosen by an act of your will to believe it, you are now ready to communicate with your heavenly Father.

Oh, you who desire a deeper walk with God, come, enter into His presence through His Word.

It is God's desire to communicate Himself to you, to impart abundant grace, and to allow you to enjoy His presence.

Three

Beginning the Journey

*L*et us begin now to practice praying the Word to God, using the Lord's Prayer in Matthew 6:9–13 as an example.

Dear reader, know this fundamental truth as you begin. When Jesus prayed for God's kingdom to come, remember that He said, *"The kingdom of God is within you"* (Luke 17:21).

Before we had invited Jesus to come into our hearts, we were lost sinners. The only promise available to us was that our wages for sin was death. (See Romans 6:23.)

But now that we have repented from our sin, turned to Christ to be cleansed from our sin, and invited Him to take up His abode with us, He has brought with Him the kingdom of God with all its benefits and promises.

Let me say something now to those in the clergy. I know many of you tell your parishioners what waits for them at the end of their earthly lives. However, you often do not give clear or sufficient instruction as to how to attain it.

Make the steps to salvation understood by even the least educated in your congregation. Their attention should be on Jesus Christ alone.

Then, teach your people, by an act of profound adoration before God, how to find Him in prayer. Tell them how to get quiet inwardly, how to keep their minds from wandering, and how to build up their faith in God through meditating on His Word.

Now, let's look together at the Lord's Prayer and ponder the meaning of the words.

Dwell on the words, *"Our Father"* (Matthew 6:9). God has taken the initiative to invite you to become His child. He desires to be your Father. Pour out your heart's desire to Him.

Now, wait a few moments in silence before Him. Always allow some quiet time as you pray in case your heavenly Father wants to reveal His will.

Come to the Father as a feeble child, soiled and bruised by repeated falls, destitute of strength to stand or of power to cleanse yourself. Allow the Father to see your confusion. Then, intermingle a word of love or grief for past sins, and sink once again into silence before Him.

Continue on in the Lord's Prayer in this same manner. Beseech the King of Glory to reign in you. Abandon yourself to God to do a finished work in you. Acknowledge His right to rule over you.

If you feel as though you should remain peaceful and quiet rather than continue on with the prayer, do so.

Then, when you are ready, continue on with the second petition, *"Thy kingdom come. Thy will be done in earth, as it is in heaven"* (Matthew 6:10). Ask God to accomplish in you and through you His will on earth. Surrender your freedom and will into His hands to be disposed of as He pleases.

When you find that it is God's will for you to be loving, you will desire to love. You will seek Him first for His love in which to love others.

Don't burden yourselves with frequent repetition of set forms or studied prayer. When you meditate on the Lord's Prayer only once and then pray it out to the Father, it will produce more fruit than meaningless repeated words.

When you come to the verse, *"Give us this day our daily bread"* (verse 11), place yourself as a sheep before your Shepherd. Look to Him for your food. "Oh, Divine Shepherd, feed Your flock with Yourself. You are indeed our daily bread."

Tell the Father all about your family's needs, but do so remembering the one great principle of faith—God is within us.

As you pray, don't form any image of God in your mind. All our imaginations of God amount to nothing. You may, however, remember Jesus Christ in His birth or crucifixion, provided you always seek Him in His resurrected state.

Perhaps, on some occasions, you come to Him needing a physician. Then, come without mental aggravation, because He has the healing virtue for all our maladies. You have no need to exert yourself in prayer. Simply yield to God's operations within you until He completes His work.

As you experiment with prayer in this manner, you will enjoy a deeper walk with God than you have ever known before. You will relish these times of rest and quiet in His presence.

It is attainable for all of you who earnestly seek God. The only requirement is to begin.

Four

The Reward of Silence

You are now ready to know about another aspect of prayer that I will simply call the prayer of faith and stillness.

After you have been meditating in the Word and praying it out to God for some time, you will gradually find how easy it is to come into His presence. You will remember other Scriptures with less difficulty. Prayer has now become easy, sweet, and delightful.

You have now found, dear one, the true way of finding God and that His *"name is as ointment poured forth"* (Song of Solomon 1:3).

Now, I want you to pray a little differently. You must now begin to use your faith and courage without being disturbed at the difficulties you may encounter.

First, as soon as you come into the presence of God, remain in respectful silence for a little while.

Remain there in His divine presence without being troubled about a subject for prayer. Simply enjoy God.

When you feel a release, you may proceed in prayer. If, however, there remains a tender tug at your Spirit to simply stay quiet in His presence, by all means do so. Cease all activity, lest God's presence is diminished by your activity.

Then I would recommend to all of you, when you have finished in prayer, remain a while longer in respectful silence.

Seek nothing from God during these quiet moments except to love Him and please Him. A servant who places all diligence in his work only for the reward is unworthy of any recompense.

Then go to your place of prayer not only to enjoy spiritual delights, but simply to please the Father.

It will keep your spirit in tranquility and consolation.

Five

Surviving Dry Periods

Although God has no other desire than to impart Himself to you, He frequently conceals Himself for a purpose. It may be to arouse you from laziness, or perhaps you have not been seeking Him in faith and love.

But for whatever reason, He does so out of His abundant goodness and faithfulness to you. Often these apparent withdrawings of Himself are followed by the caresses of His love.

During these seasons, you may begin to believe that the way to prove your faith is by a greater degree of affection or by an exertion of strength and activity. Surely, you may say this will induce God to revisit you.

No, dear soul, believe me, this is not the way. You must await the return of the Beloved with patient love, humility, peace, and silent worship.

By doing these things, you demonstrate to the Father that it is Himself alone and His good pleasure that you seek and not the selfish delights of your own satisfaction.

Don't be impatient in your times of dryness. Wait patiently for God. In doing so, your prayer life will increase and be renewed.

In abandonment and contentment, learn to wait for the return of your Beloved. Intermingle your waiting with sighs of love. This conduct will indeed please God and compel His return.

Six

The Road to Perfection

I now want you to begin to learn how to abandon yourself—your entire existence—to God. Every moment of every day you must come to realize that you are in God's immediate will.

Knowing and understanding this conviction of abandonment will cause you to regard everything that comes your way as being from the hand of the Father.

Dearly beloved, once you have given yourself to God, do not take yourself back again. Remember, a gift once presented is no longer at the disposal of the giver.

Abandonment is a matter of great importance in our progress. It is the key to the inner court. He who knows how to abandon himself to God is on his way to perfection.

Therefore, don't listen to other confusing voices of natural reason. Remain steadfast. Great faith produces great abandonment.

Be like Abraham, *"who against hope believed in hope"* (Romans 4:18).

Abandonment means casting off all selfish cares in order to be altogether at His divine disposal. Each of us is exhorted to abandonment.

"Take therefore no thought for the morrow" (Matthew 6:34), *"for your heavenly Father knoweth that ye have need of all these things"* (verse 32).

"In all thy ways acknowledge him, and he shall direct thy paths" (Proverbs 3:6).

"Commit thy works unto the LORD, and thy thoughts shall be established" (Proverbs 16:3).

"Commit thy way unto the LORD; trust also in him; and he shall bring it to pass" (Psalm 37:5).

You must give up both the external and the internal things—all of your concerns must be placed into the hands of God. Forget yourself. Think only of Him. In doing so, your heart will remain free and at peace.

It is essential to continually submit your will to God's will and renounce every private inclination as soon as it arises—no matter how good it appears. You must want only what God has willed from all eternity. Forget the past. Devote the present to God. Be satisfied with the present moment that brings God's eternal order to you. Attribute nothing that happens to you as coming from man, but regard everything, except sin, as coming from God.

Surrender yourself to be led and disposed of as God pleases in respect to your outward and inward state.

Seven

The Bitter and the Sweet

Be patient, dear ones, during suffering. It was through His suffering on Calvary that Jesus gave the greatest display of love.

Don't be like those who give themselves to Jesus at one season only to withdraw from Him at another. They give themselves to Him only to be caressed, yet in times of trouble they turn back to man for consolation.

No, beloved friends, you will not find consolation in anything other than the love of the cross and total abandonment. If you will not savor the cross, you cannot savor the things of God. (See Matthew 16:23.)

It is impossible to love God without loving the cross. If you savor the cross, you will find even the most bitter things to be sweet.

"To the hungry soul every bitter thing is sweet" (Proverbs 27:7), because it finds itself hungering

for God in the same proportion as it is hungering for the cross.

God gives us the cross, which gives us God. Abandonment and the cross go hand in hand.

As soon as anything is presented to you in the form of suffering, and you begin to feel resistance in your spirit, resign yourself immediately to God. Give yourself and your circumstances to Him in sacrifice.

Then, when the cross arrives, it will not be so very burdensome because you have submitted yourself to it. I do not mean, however, that you will not feel the weight of the cross. If you do not feel the cross, you do not suffer. A responsiveness to suffering is one of the principal parts of suffering itself.

Jesus Christ Himself chose to endure the utmost severity of the cross.

Sometimes we bear the cross in weakness and at other times in strength, yet it is all the same will of God for us.

Abandon yourself to God, trust Him, and He will bring about good toward you and glory for Him.

Jesus said, *"I am the way, the truth, and the life: no man cometh unto the Father, but by me"* (John 14:6).

Abandon yourself, then, in Jesus. Follow Him as the way. Wait for Him to reveal truth to you. Allow Him to animate you with life.

Abandonment is the means God uses to reveal His mysteries to us.

To bear all the marks of Jesus Christ is much greater than merely meditating on them. Paul said, *"I bear in my body the marks of the Lord Jesus"* (Galatians 6:17). He did not say he merely thought about them; he said he bore them.

As you abandon yourselves to Jesus, He will reveal those marks to you. You have no choice but to reach after Him. Dwell with Him. Sink into nothingness before Him.

Accept indiscriminately all His gifts, whether sweetness or bitterness. Let nothing slow down your course for even one moment.

God may take some of you aside for years at a time to reveal the enjoyment of one single mystery. Walk, then, in the light He has given you.

But if God chooses to withdraw this illumination from you, be just as willing to yield it back to Him.

I know that some of you may feel incapable at first of meditating on the mysteries God reveals to you in His Word. But don't be afraid to enter into all that God has for you.

If you sincerely love God, you will love all that belongs to Him.

Eight

Transforming Love

*S*t. Augustine once said, "Love God, and then do what you please." If you will obey the commandment of Jesus to *"love the Lord thy God with all thy heart, and with all thy soul, and with all thy mind....And...thy neighbour as thyself"* (Matthew 22:37–39), then you will be assured that you are praying in God's will.

You know that when you love someone, you want only the best for that person. Hurting or offending your loved one never enters your mind.

Well, love is manifested in your life as a result of your closeness to God. For He is *all love*.

When God comes to live within us, He brings with Him all of His virtues—all of His goodness. The more we allow Him to possess us, the more we possess His superior goodness and love.

For love to be genuine and permanent, you must possess God's characteristics. By His grace, He must give these to you, or your own human love is like a mask that you use for appearance only. *"The king's daughter is all glorious within"* (Psalm 45:13).

God is exceedingly jealous over His children. He does not permit them to walk in falsehood. Those who know God practice His superior love toward others without conscious effort. It becomes natural to them.

If divine love glows within you, you will not try to flee suffering and adversity. You will think of only how to please your Beloved in that circumstance.

Forget yourself and your own personal ambitions. Let your love for God increase. In so doing, you will learn to love the Creator more than the created.

Dear ones, how simple this truth is. Even the uneducated may learn to live in love.

My own heart is burdened when I think how easily the entire church could be transformed if only they would love. But will they?

Will you?

Nine

Put Off the Old

I now want to address those dear souls who are still having problems with their old self-nature and its desires.

Don't be discouraged.

Scripture tells us that when God came to live within us by the Holy Spirit, we *"put off the old man with his deeds; and have put on the new man, which is renewed in knowledge after the image of him that created him"* (Colossians 3:9–10).

You will find yourself warring against your own fleshly nature as long as you are still in your human body. It is almost impossible to acquire total death to your senses and passions.

The reason is obvious. While still in your human body, your soulish desires give energy to your senses. Your senses stimulate your passions. A dead body has no sensations and desires nothing.

All attempts to correct the external only drive the soul into more furious activity. Rather than overcome the problems the old self-nature imposes, a flurry of activity only seems to cause fragmented lives redirected into harsh feelings about yourself.

Depending upon your senses for guidance only provokes and stirs up your passions within. The more you place your focus on the self-nature activities, the more they seem to thrive and grow.

Harshness and denial of pleasures may only serve to weaken your body rather than dull or eliminate the activity of your senses.

The only genuine means of bringing about change is by inward means. You must commit yourself wholly into the hands of a loving God. The simple act of commitment in every circumstance where self exerts itself will, in time, produce a separation of the carnal from the spiritual.

The nearer your spirit draws to God, the further you become separated from the soulish demands. When God responds to your yielding desires by sending His grace, your outward nature, your self-nature, is weakened and easily complies to God's will.

Now, let me say something about being introspective. Dying to your self-nature is a command from God. It plays a vital part in your relationship with Him and with others.

However, a constant, inward gaze should never be a primary, principal exercise of a

Christian. Your main focus should always be on God and the activities involved in getting to know Him.

God Himself will show you the areas of your life that need attention. Those who are faithfully abandoning all to God will indeed be purified, polished, and perfected in His timing.

Our responsibility is to remain steadfast in our attention toward God; then things will be done in perfection.

Every believer is capable of maturing in God in this manner.

Your busy imagination will continually supply you with the danger of falling into excessive activity of dying to self, but God will teach you if you will only follow the Holy Spirit's promptings.

The rewards for this method are great. You will constantly find yourself relying on God, and you will learn the secrets of His sustaining and preserving power. You will also achieve the end result of being removed from your sin nature.

Ten

The Central Force

*Turn ye unto him from whom the children of Israel
have deeply revolted.*
—Isaiah 31:6

Conversion is nothing more than turning from yourself in order to return to God. It has nothing to do with the outward nature of good works. Conversion takes place within the spirit of a man.

Once you have made a decision to know God, you will find that God has placed a desire in your heart to continually draw nearer to Him. The closer you grow to God, the stronger the desire becomes. It becomes natural, almost habitual, to place God at the center of your life.

Let me assure you that it is only by divine grace that we are able to know God. You must never presume that it is by your own efforts. You are not capable of coming to God unless He has chosen to call you first. *"Ye have not chosen me, but I have chosen you"* (John 15:16).

You must simply follow the desires of your heart to know God, turn from the wickedness of the world, and continue firmly in your walk with Him.

God has an attractive virtue that will more and more powerfully draw you to Himself. As He draws, He also purifies. The sun draws water from the earth, and the water must simply remain passive. So you, too, must freely and voluntarily be drawn to God.

God is our center. The center always exerts a powerful attraction. The more spiritual and exalted our center is, the more irresistible is its attractiveness.

When your spirit has been united with God's, it will fall without any force other than the weight of love into its proper center. The more peaceful and trusting you remain, the more rapidly you will advance because self-energy will not obstruct you.

Take care then, dear one, to direct your attention toward God.

Do not be discouraged by difficulties you may encounter as you press on to know God. He will soon reward you with abundant supplies of grace, provided you are faithful in returning to Him who is your center.

Hereafter, *"when the enemy shall come in like a flood, the Spirit of the LORD shall lift up a standard against him"* (Isaiah 59:19).

Eleven

Entering into Effortless Prayer

*H*ave you been faithful to incorporate into your prayer life what you have been learning in this little book? Are you gradually sensing God's presence more and more with you as you kneel in prayer?

Good! Because you should soon enjoy a continual sense of God's presence that will become natural for you. His presence, as well as prayer, should soon become almost habitual to you. You should be aware of an unusual serenity that comes over you in prayer.

This, dear one, is indeed God communicating His love to you. It is the beginning of the blessedness too great to describe.

Oh, how I would love to pursue this subject and to continue to share with you what progress can be made in experiencing God through prayer! But I am writing basically for beginners; and, in the Lord's timing, you will experience all that God has for you.

It is important now that you cease from self-action and self-exertion in attempting to experience His presence. God Himself can act alone.

God said to David, *"Be still, and know that I am God"* (Psalm 46:10).

We, the created, sometimes become so infatuated with love and attachment to our own works that we walk in disbelief unless we can feel, know, and distinguish the completed work.

God's operations, His manner, and His swiftness are simply unable to be discerned. As the Creator's workings abound more and more with us, they will absorb our own self-efforts.

It seems as though the stars shine more brightly before the sun rises and gradually vanish as the light advances. They have not really become invisible. A greater light has simply absorbed the lesser light.

This is also the case with your self-effort in prayer. Since God's light is so much greater, it absorbs our little flickers of activity. They will grow faint and eventually disappear until all self-effort to experience God is no longer distinguishable.

I have heard the accusation from some that this is a "prayer of inactivity." They are wrong. Such charges come from the inexperienced. Those who have attained God's presence in prayer by relinquishing self-effort can address this question because they are full of light and knowledge.

Indeed, those who have experienced God have done so because God had first chosen to meet with them. No amount of self-effort will bring you into His presence.

The fullness of grace will still the activity of self. Therefore, it is of the utmost importance that you remain as silent as possible.

When an infant draws milk from his mother, he begins by moving his little mouth and lips. But once his nourishment begins to flow abundantly, he then remains quite content to swallow without any further effort.

This is how we must act in the beginning of our prayer. Move your lips in praise and in affection; but as soon as the milk of divine grace flows freely, in stillness, take it in. When it ceases to flow, again stir up your affection as the infant moves his lips.

Do not force into this beautiful act of grace the multiplicity of self!

Who could believe that gently and without exertion we can receive our nourishment, just as a babe receives his milk? Yet the more peaceful a child remains, the more nourishment he receives. He may even fall asleep while nursing.

This is how your spirit should be in prayer: peaceful, relaxed, and without effort.

God's presence is not a stronghold to be taken by force or violence. His is a kingdom of peace, which can only be gained through love. God demands nothing extraordinary or difficult. On the contrary, He is greatly pleased by simple, childlike conduct.

The most glorious attainments in prayer are those that are most easily reached. If you want to reach the ocean, sail a boat down the river. Eventually, without exertion or effort, you will find the greater waters.

Are you ready now to find God? Are you willing to follow this sweet and simple path? If your answer is yes, then you will surely find your object of destination.

Oh, just once try this way of prayer. Soon you will find that your own experience will carry you infinitely beyond what my few words have taught you.

What is it that you fear?

Why don't you instantly cast yourself into the arms of Jesus, who extended His arms on the cross so that He might embrace you?

What risk do you run in abandoning yourself wholly to Him?

Oh, Jesus will not deceive you; He will only bestow on you a greater abundance than you have ever hoped for.

Those who lean toward their own understanding and their own self-effort may hear this rebuke of God spoken by his prophet Isaiah: "You have wearied yourselves in the multiplicity of your ways, and have not said, let us rest in peace." (See Isaiah 57:10.)

Twelve

Remaining Quiet in God's Presence

*I*f you have followed me through the preceding chapters, and you have practiced the various methods of experiencing God, you are now ready for the most simplistic exercise of all.

It is one of entering into God's presence as I have described to you and remaining quiet.

You should be aware of God's presence, without interruption, throughout your entire day. As soon as your eyes close in prayer, you should be blessed by the joy of communion with Him in which external events cannot interrupt.

Being in His presence will make you sweetly submissive to His goodness and grace—insensible to all evil. Don't hurry into other forms of prayer when you are quiet before God. Simply allow yourself time to enjoy His presence and be filled full in your spirit.

"But the LORD *is in his holy temple: let all the earth keep silence before him"* (Habakkuk 2:20).

God's Word is essential and eternal.

As you remain quiet, the presence of His Word in your spirit is in some degree a capacity for the reception of Himself.

Perhaps it is during this time of silence that God may choose to speak to you. Hearing is a passive rather than an active procedure. Rest. Rest. Rest in God's love. The only work you are required to do now is to give your most intense attention to His still, small voice within.

Scripture exhorts us to be attentive to the voice of God. *"My sheep hear my voice, and I know them, and they follow me"* (John 10:27).

"Hearken unto me, my people; and give ear unto me, O my nation" (Isaiah 51:4).

"Hearken, O daughter, and consider, and incline thine ear; forget also thine own people, and thy father's house; so shall the king greatly desire thy beauty: for he is thy Lord; and worship thou him" (Psalm 45:10–11).

Forget about yourself and all your household and occupational interests. Simply listen and be attentive to God. These passive actions will permit God to communicate His love to you.

Being internally occupied with God is wholly incompatible with being externally busied by a thousand trivialities.

You should repeat the process of becoming internally quiet as often as distractions occur. It is really not much to ask of ourselves to take an hour or even a half hour from our day to quiet our spirits in order for the spirit of prayer to remain with us the entire day.

Thirteen

Examine Yourself

*I*n this chapter, I would like to teach you how to examine yourselves in confession. Self-examination should always precede confession.

There is the danger, however, in self-examination, of depending on the diligence of our own scrutiny rather than on God for the discovery and knowledge of our sins. This examination should be peaceful and tranquil.

When we examine ourselves with effort, we can easily be deceived and betrayed because self-love can lead us into error.

"Woe unto them that call evil good, and good evil" (Isaiah 5:20).

When we lie in full exposure before Jesus, the *"Sun of righteousness"* (Malachi 4:2), His divine beams render the smallest atoms visible.

Abandon yourself, then, in examination as well as confession, to God.

When you are accustomed to this type of surrender, you will find that as soon as a fault is committed, God will rebuke it through an inward burning. He allows no evil to be concealed in the lives of His children. The only way to deal with this is to turn simply to God and bear the pain and correction He inflicts.

Since He is to become the incessant examiner of your soul, you can no longer have the job of examining yourself. If you are faithful in your abandonment to God in this area, your experiences will prove that exploration by His divine light is more effective than your own careful examination.

If you will walk this way, you must be informed of a matter in which you are most likely to err. When you begin to give an account for your sins, instead of the regret and contrition you have been accustomed to feel, you will now begin to experience tranquility, and love will take possession of your spirit.

If you are not properly instructed, you will resist this experience because you have, up to this time, been taught that contrition is required of you.

But genuine contrition, infused with God's love, infinitely surpasses any effect produced by self-exertion. Your contrition and God's love combine in one principal act to a higher perfection than ever known before.

God acts so excellently in us and for us. To hate sin is to hate it as God does. His purest love acts immediately in our spirits when needed. Why, then, are you so eager for any action other than this?

Put your confidence in God, and remain quiet where He has placed you. You will soon be amazed at the difficulty you have in calling your faults to remembrance. Don't let this cause you to have a moment's uneasiness. Forgetting your faults is proof of your having been purified from them. It is best to forget whatever concerns you so that you may remember only God.

Second, because confession is our duty before God, He will not fail to make known to us our greatest faults.

At the end of God's examinations, we will feel as though more has been accomplished than could ever possibly have been through all our own endeavors.

For those of you who have diligently followed along through these chapters and have begun to put my teaching into practice, I exhort you to continue on.

God Himself will be your reward.

Fourteen

Distractions

*P*erhaps now is a good time to deal with the problem of distraction while trying to pray. No matter how sincere you are about praying, there will come a time when your mind wanders and it seems impossible not to be distracted.

Let me give you an important principle. Don't struggle with your temptations or distractions. It only seems to increase their intensity and draw you away from your sole purpose of seeking God.

Simply turn away from the evil and draw nearer to God.

If a little child fears an imaginary monster, he does not stand up to fight it. Instead, he closes his eyes to it and shrinks into the bosom of his mother for safety.

"God is in the midst of her; she shall not be moved: God shall help her, and that right early" (Psalm 46:5).

If in our weakness we attempt to attack the enemies of our soul, we will find ourselves wounded, if not defeated. But by remaining in the simple presence of God, we will find an instant supply of strength and support.

David knew this to be his source of strength. He said, *"Therefore my heart is glad, and my glory rejoiceth: my flesh also shall rest in hope"* (Psalm 16:9).

Exodus 14:14 tells us, *"The LORD shall fight for you, and ye shall hold your peace."*

Be careful also not to allow your mind to dwell much on your weaknesses and unworthiness. These excessive feelings spring from a root of pride and a love for our own excellence.

To become discouraged weakens your prayer life, and this is worse than your imperfections themselves. The more miserable you see yourself, the more it should cause you to abandon yourself to God.

Press in to have a more intimate relationship with Him.

God Himself said, *"I will instruct thee and teach thee in the way which thou shalt go: I will guide thee with mine eye"* (Psalm 32:8).

Fifteen

The Formal Prayer

On occasion it may be helpful to you to open before you in prayer a book of written petitions. I would not, however, recommend it as a constant practice.

Read a little. Just enough to collect your own thoughts. But always stop when the Holy Spirit within quickens you to your own prayer.

It is necessary to vocalize all prayer. If you are praying aloud, and it becomes burdensome to you, yield to your internal drawing and remain silent in prayer—unless, of course, you are in a position with others where you are obligated to vocal prayer.

In any case, what I want to impress upon you is not to become burdened by any one form of prayer. Don't allow yourself to be tied down to the repetition of set forms. It is far better to be wholly led by the Holy Spirit in prayer, for then all aspects of the prayer will be complete.

Don't be surprised when former methods of prayer are no longer comfortable to you.

Now, the Holy Spirit will make intercession through you according to the will of God. He will help you in your infirmities, *"for we know not what we should pray for as we ought: but the Spirit itself maketh intercession for us with groanings which cannot be uttered"* (Romans 8:26).

God's design for our lives must take first place. This should strip us of all our own actions so that His plan may be substituted in their place.

Allow this work, then, to be done in you. Don't become attached to any form of formal prayer no matter how good it may appear. It is no longer good for you if it turns you aside from what God desires of you.

Shake off all self-interest and live by faith and abandonment. It is here that genuine faith truly begins to operate.

Sixteen

Sacrificial Praying

*And another angel came and stood at the altar,
having a golden censer; and there was given unto
him much incense, that he should offer it with the
prayers of all saints upon the golden altar
which was before the throne.*
—Revelation 8:3

According to John, the beloved disciple of Jesus, prayer is an incense that ascends to God. It is simply pouring out the contents of one's heart in the presence of God. *"I...have poured out my soul before the LORD"* (1 Samuel 1:15), said the mother of Samuel.

When the warmth of God's love melts and dissolves your spirit, it causes your prayer to ascend unto God in a sweet aroma.

A good illustration of this is found in Song of Solomon 1:12. The spouse says, *"While the king setteth at his table, my spikenard sendeth forth the smell thereof."* The table is representative of the center of your spirit. When God is there, and you know how to abide with Him, His sacred presence gradually dissolves the hardness of your heart.

The beloved says of his spouse, *"Who is this that cometh out of the wilderness like pillars of smoke, perfumed with myrrh and frankincense?"* (Song of Solomon 3:6).

Your spirit ascends to God by giving itself up to the annihilating powers of divine love.

This is a state of sacrifice essential to the Christian life. Allowing God's will, God's desire, and God's Word to be first gives honor to the sovereignty of God. When self-interests have been destroyed, you have, in the truest sense, acknowledged the supreme existence of God.

In order that the Spirit of the eternal Word may exist in us, we must give up our lives as He Himself lives in us.

Perhaps these words I write seem strange to you. Let me refer you to Scripture again so that you may better understand the sacrifice of self to God.

Colossians 3:3 says, *"For ye are dead, and your life is hid with Christ in God."*

This does not mean that your physical body is dead. It means you have, in sacrificial giving, forsaken yourself to be lost in Jesus. Then you can say along with the apostle John, *"Blessing, and honour, and glory, and power, be unto him that sitteth upon the throne, and unto the Lamb for ever and ever"* (Revelation 5:13).

One of the greatest secrets to experiencing God in prayer is this: *"True worshippers shall worship the Father in spirit and in truth"* (John 4:23). This worship is *"in spirit"* because you are drawn away from your own carnal, human methods into the purity of the Spirit within you; and it is *"in truth"* because you are in Christ, and in Him is all truth.

Have you been praying this way? Have you been pouring yourself at the feet of Jesus in sacrificial prayer? I'm positive that as soon as you begin, you will find that God will instantly fill you with Himself.

Ah, if only you knew the blessings you would derive from praying in this manner, you would never again be satisfied to pray as you once did.

Finding the kingdom of God is like finding a *"treasure hid in a field"* (Matthew 13:44) or like finding a *"pearl of great price"* (verse 46). It is *"living water"* (John 4:10) and *"everlasting life"* (verse 14).

But the most wonderful truth of all is that Jesus assures us that this *"kingdom of God is within you"* (Luke 17:21). How can this be? How can this valuable treasure be found in us?

In two ways—first, when we surrender to God and ask Him to be our Lord, letting nothing resist His dominion, He comes to dwell within us; then, having possession of God, who is the Supreme Good, we possess His kingdom in which lies all the fullness of joy.

The ultimate purpose for each of us who knows God is to love Him and enjoy His presence.

What a shame that we forget the simplicity of this great truth!

Seventeen

How to Be Led by the Spirit

J would now like to introduce you to one
of the primary goals in prayer—to be led
by the Spirit of God.

In previous chapters, I asked you to consider
the benefits of remaining silent before God. I
hope you have been practicing this in your time
of prayer. Remember, it does not mean that you
remain dull and inactive. But rather the activity
within your spirit is now being moved by God
Himself through the agency of His Spirit.

Paul exhorted us to be *"led by the Spirit of
God"* (Romans 8:14).

Ezekiel, the prophet, had a vision of wheels
that had a living Spirit within. Wherever the
Spirit went, they went. They ascended and de-
scended as the Spirit of life directed. (See Ezekiel 1:20–21.)

We, in like manner, must move according
to the life-giving Spirit within us and be cau-
tiously faithful to move only when He moves.

Therefore, your actions will not reflect on you but rather the Creator who made you and desires to lead you throughout your entire life.

This "activity" of being led will always surround you with peace. When you interrupt the Spirit's leading, you will always sense it because you will feel either forced or constrained. But when your actions are under the influence of the Spirit of grace, they will be free, easy, and so natural that it will almost seem as though you have not acted at all.

Psalm 18:19 says, *"He brought me forth also into a large place; he delivered me, because he delighted in me."*

When your spirit is centered on God, all activities He initiates will be noble, full of peace, natural, and so spontaneous that it will appear to you there has hardly been any activity at all.

For instance, watch a wheel while it rolls slowly by. Can't you easily see all its parts? But when it rapidly passes by, you can distinguish nothing.

Beloved, when you are at rest in God, your activity, while being magnificently uplifting, will also be altogether peaceful. And the more peaceful it is, the more will be accomplished, because it is God who is moving and directing your actions.

God Himself draws us. He causes us to run after Him.

In the first chapter of the Song of Solomon, the spouse speaks to her beloved and says, *"Draw me"* (verse 4). We, too, can say, "Draw me, O Lord, unto Yourself. You are my divine center. You hold the secret to my very existence, and I will follow You."

God's attraction is both a perfume to allure and an ointment to heal. Yet each soul is given the freedom without constraint to follow Him. God never uses force. Instead, He attracts us by His powerful sweet presence.

O God, draw us; draw us ever closer to You by the power of Your sweet Holy Spirit.

Eighteen

Divine Dependence

I hope you have understood my emphasis thus far of learning to rely on God for even the slightest spiritual activity. It certainly is not my intention to promote a lazy, dull existence. Our highest form of activity is to press on into a total dependence on the Spirit of God.

"For in him we live, and move, and have our being" (Acts 17:28).

This submissive dependence on the Spirit of God is indispensably necessary and will cause your spirit to attain unity and simplicity with God as He created it to.

Having discussed the need to be led by the Spirit in previous chapters, let us now go on to forsake the various activities we have acclimated into our prayer lives and enter into the simplicity and unity of God in whose image we were originally formed. (See Genesis 1:27.)

Entering into unity with God means being wholly united to His Holy Spirit. By this means, we have one and the same Spirit with Him. Without any effort on our part, we are then placed in a position for God's will to work through us.

Oh, hallelujah! Just think of it! When we are wholly influenced by the Spirit of God, who is infinitely active, our activity will indeed be more energetic, more vibrant than anything we could ever initiate within ourselves.

Yield yourself to the guidance of His wisdom. *"If any of you lack wisdom, let him ask of God"* (James 1:5). Then trust in the wisdom God gives you, and you will begin to see your efforts bearing fruit.

"All things were made by him; and without him was not any thing made that was made" (John 1:3).

God formed us originally in His own image and likeness. He breathed into us that *"breath of life"* (Genesis 2:7). This life was to be simple, pure, intimate, and always fruitful.

However, Satan deformed the divine image in our spirits through sin. Now, through the Word of God, the Holy Spirit refreshes, renews, and renovates our broken spirits.

Since the Holy Spirit is the express image of God the Father, it is necessary that He alone work in us. His image could not be formed in us by our own effort. This is why we must remain passive in the hands of the Workman.

Place yourself in a position of quietness to receive from God. Remain pliable and open to the operations of the eternal Word.

Have you ever seen a painter able to produce a perfect picture while working on top of an unsteady table? No, I'm sure you have not. So, too, in your life, every movement of "self" produces erroneous lines, interrupting the work and defeating the design of our adorable Painter.

Remain in peace. Move only when Jesus does. In Jesus there is life (see John 5:26), and He must give life to every living thing.

The Spirit within the church is divine. He is not idle, barren, or unfruitful. His activity is solely dependent upon God who moves and governs. Those who are in the church are spiritual children who must also move only by the promptings of the Spirit.

Actions produced by a divine principle are divine; but creature actions, however good they appear, are still only human. Any virtue in them is only because of divine grace.

Jesus Christ tells us that there is life only in Himself. All other human beings have only a borrowed life. Jesus desires to bestow this life upon mankind. By rejecting the self-life and suppressing its activity, you will have opened the door and made room for the Master.

"Therefore, if any man be in Christ, he is a new creature: old things are passed away; behold, all things are become new" (2 Corinthians 5:17).

Do you desire old things to become new? Set aside your own activities so that God's activities may be substituted in their place.

Man is by nature restless and turbulent. He does little, though it appears to be much. Jesus rebuked Martha even though what she was doing had the appearance of good. *"Martha, Martha,"* Jesus said, *"thou art careful and troubled about many things: but one thing is needful: and Mary hath chosen that good part, which shall not be taken away from her"* (Luke 10:41–42).

What had Mary chosen? Rest, tranquility, and peace. She had ceased to act in order for the Spirit of Christ to act in her.

Renounce yourself and all your own activities. Follow Jesus. You cannot do so by being animated by your own spirit.

Paul said, *"But he that is joined unto the Lord is one spirit"* (1 Corinthians 6:17). David said, *"It is good for me to draw near to God"* (Psalm 73:28).

What are the advantages of being joined to and drawn near to the Lord? They are the beginning of an everlasting union with God the Father.

What could satisfy creatures more than an eternal presence with the Creator?

Nineteen

The Holy Spirit in Prayer

*I*t is of vital importance for you to read carefully the Scripture verses in this chapter. God has revealed to His children the secret of effective prayer by telling us how He actually assists in prayer through His Holy Spirit.

"Now if any man have not the Spirit of Christ, he is none of his" (Romans 8:9).

To belong to Jesus, we must be filled with His Spirit and emptied of our own.

The apostle Paul knew the necessity of the divine influence of the Spirit in his life. In verse fourteen he continued, *"For as many as are led by the Spirit of God, they are the sons of God."* Divine outworking must first have divine infilling.

Again, he said, *"For ye have not received the spirit of bondage again to fear; but ye have received the Spirit of adoption, whereby we cry, Abba, Father"* (Romans 8:15).

The Spirit Paul spoke of is none other than the actual Spirit of Jesus Christ who comes to us, lives in and through us, and helps us to experience the presence of God. His Spirit brings assurance that we are no longer children of the world, but we now belong to God.

"The Spirit itself beareth witness with our spirit, that we are the children of God" (verse 16).

Do you desire this oneness with God? Is your soul hungering and thirsting for this union with Him?

Then, dear one of God, yield yourself now to the influence of this blessed Spirit of Christ. Allow yourself to receive the truth of God's Word that He will indeed fill you full of Himself. With joy, receive the Spirit of liberty, which only belongs to the children of God, and put off the *"spirit of bondage"* (verse 15).

Allow your spirit to be set free—energized with enthusiasm for the things of God.

Paul wrote plainly so that all might understand this vital secret of prayer. *"Likewise the Spirit also helpeth our infirmities: for we know not what we should pray for as we ought: but the Spirit itself maketh intercession for us with groanings which cannot be uttered"* (verse 26).

God spoke through Paul so that we would not be ignorant of spiritual things. He wanted us to know of the Holy Spirit's intercession through us as we pray. We do not stand alone before God. What blessed hope and comfort this gives us!

Since God knows what we have need of, and His Spirit is within us, shouldn't we then permit Him to pour out His unutterable groanings on our behalf?

Jesus Himself said to the Father, *"I knew that thou hearest me always"* (John 11:42). If we freely allow His Spirit to pray and intercede for us, we also will always be heard.

Why? Listen again to Paul, who mastered this secret: *"He that searcheth the hearts knoweth what is the mind of the Spirit, because he maketh intercession for the saints according to the will of God"* (Romans 8:27).

What he was saying is simply that the Spirit of God prays only in accordance with the will of God. God's will is that every man should be saved and that we may become perfect. The Spirit therefore intercedes for all that is necessary for our perfection.

Why, then, are you burdened with the cares of this world? Why do you weary yourself in the multiplicity of your ways without ever saying, "I will rest in His peace"?

God invites you to cast all your cares upon Him, *"for he careth for you"* (1 Peter 5:7).

His heart must have been filled with great sorrow as He looked upon His created, who was exhausting all his strength on a thousand external objects when there was so little to do to attain all he desired. *"Wherefore,"* God said, *"do ye spend money for that which is not bread? and your labour for that which satisfieth not? hearken diligently unto me, and eat ye that which is good, and let your soul delight itself in fatness"* (Isaiah 55:2).

Oh, that we would know the blessedness of "hearkening diligently" unto God! How greatly our souls would be strengthened by such direction!

"Be silent, O all flesh before the Lord" (Zechariah 2:13). Cease from laboring in prayer as soon as you sense the prompting of the Spirit of God to pray through you.

God assures us that we need to fear nothing. He promises to take very special care of us.

"Can a woman forget her sucking child, that she should not have compassion on the son of her womb? yea, they may forget, yet will I not forget thee. Behold, I have graven thee upon the palms of my hands; thy walls are continually before me" (Isaiah 49:15–16).

After reading these beautiful words of consolation, how can you ever again be afraid to abandon yourself wholly to the guidance of God?

Twenty

Matters of the Heart

*O*ne of the first things you will begin to experience in your newly discovered ways of prayer will be a desire to share this with others. Let me prepare you and assure you that your labors are not in vain.

Anyone who labors for the conversion of others must first reach them by way of their hearts. If those you love and are witnessing to are introduced immediately to the secrets of prayer and how to experience God through prayer, I assure you permanent conversions will result.

Little fruit will be found in a person if you disciple him into many burdensome, external exercises of leading him into the knowledge of *"Christ in you, the hope of glory"* (Colossians 1:27).

You who are ministers must instruct your flock to experience the presence of God within. In this way, the farmer at his plow may have blessed sweet communion with his God. The laborer, while exhausted in his outward man from his labors, may be renewed in his inner man with strength. All manner of sin and temptation will soon disappear and you, O minister, will have spiritually-minded men.

Once you have gained admission to another's heart, you can easily discuss matters pertaining to the spirit. This is why God, above all things, requires the heart. By this means alone, we can destroy the dreadful sins of drunkenness, blasphemy, lewdness, and theft. Jesus Christ would reign everywhere in peace, and the church would be renewed throughout.

The decay of internal holiness is unquestionably the source of many sins that have appeared in the world. All these would be overthrown if inward devotion were reestablished.

Sin takes possession of the soul deficient in faith and prayer. If we would only teach our wandering brothers and sisters to simply believe and diligently pray, rather than engaging them in endless reasonings, we would lead them sweetly into the arms of God.

Oh, how inexpressibly great is the loss sustained by the man who neglects his inner spiritual man! What an account will those have to give who are entrusted with the care of souls, yet have not communicated this hidden treasure to their flock.

Some of you will excuse yourselves by saying that there is danger in this way or that simple persons are incapable of comprehending the things of the spirit.

But Scripture affirms, *"The testimony of the LORD is sure, making wise the simple"* (Psalm 19:7).

What danger can there be in walking in the true ways of Jesus Christ, giving ourselves up to Him, fixing our eyes continually on Him, placing all our confidence in His grace, and giving all the strength of our souls to His purest love?

The simple ones are far from incapable of this perfection. By their gentleness, innocence, and humility, they are especially qualified for this achievement; and as they are not accustomed to reasoning out every detail, they are less obstinate in their opinions. Those who are cramped and blinded by self-sufficiency offer much greater resistance to the operation of grace.

"The entrance of thy words giveth light: it giveth understanding unto the simple" (Psalm 119:130), said the psalmist.

Spiritual fathers, be careful that you do not prevent your little ones from coming to Christ. Jesus said to the apostles, *"Suffer little children, and forbid them not, to come unto me: for of such is the kingdom of heaven"* (Matthew 19:14). Even the youngest child may experience God. Jesus chided His apostles when children were held away from Him.

How often we have applied a bandage to our outward bodies while the disease lies in our hearts! The reason we have been largely unsuccessful in reforming mankind is that we have dealt with external matters rather than internal. If we deal first with the matters of the heart, the outward concerns will follow quite naturally.

To teach a man to seek God in his heart, to think of Him, to return to Him whenever he has wandered, and to have a single focus on pleasing Him, is leading that person to the source of all grace. There he will find everything necessary for sanctification.

I beseech you all, especially those in charge of other souls, teach them at once the way of Jesus Christ. No, not I, but Jesus Himself calls you to this by the very blood He has shed for those entrusted to you.

Oh, you who dispense His grace—you preachers of His Word, you ministers of His sacraments—establish His kingdom! Make Him ruler over the heart, for it is in the heart where opposition or subjection occurs.

Teach the young to pray, not by reasoning or by method or by understanding, but by the prayer from the heart—the prayer of God's Spirit rather than man's invention.

Directing them to pray in elaborate forms will create huge obstacles. By endeavoring to teach them the refined language of prayer, you will have led them astray.

Go, then, you poor children, to your heavenly Father. Speak in your natural language. Although it may be simple and crude to you, it is not so to Him. An earthly father is more pleased to be addressed with love and respect because it comes from the heart rather than with dry, barren, elaborate words. Undisguised emotions of love are infinitely more expressive than all language or reasoning.

Men have desired to love by formal rules and have instead lost much of that love. Oh, how necessary it is to teach the art of loving!

There is no better way to learn how to love God than to simply love Him.

The Spirit of God needs none of our arranging. When it pleases Him, He turns shepherds into prophets. He throws wide the gates to the temple of prayer. He cries aloud in the highway, *"Whoso is simple, let him turn in hither"* (Proverbs 9:4).

I conclude this chapter with words from Jesus Himself. He lifted His prayer to heaven and said, *"I thank thee, O Father, Lord of heaven and earth, because thou hast hid these things from the wise and prudent, and hast revealed them unto babes"* (Matthew 11:25).

Twenty-one

The Ultimate Goal

We have traveled together through many pages on our journey toward experiencing God through prayer. What, then, is our ultimate end?

It is to be united with God in divine union forever.

However, none of the ways I have suggested are an end in themselves. Whenever all has been said and done, what still remains is the fact that God is God. All that is of man and his own doing, be it ever so noble, must first be destroyed.

All efforts—no, the very existence—of self must be destroyed. Nothing opposes God more than self. The purity of your spirit will increase in proportion as it loses its selfhood. By departing from selfhood, you will have acquired the purity and innocence of God.

To unite two things so opposite as the purity of God and the impurity of the creature, the simplicity of God and the multiplicity of man, much more is required than the efforts of the creature.

Nothing less than an operation of the Almighty can ever accomplish this, because two things must have similarity before they can become one. The impurity of dross cannot be united with the purity of gold.

How, then, does God purify? He sends His own Wisdom before Him as fire to destroy all impure activity. Nothing can resist the power of that fire. It consumes everything. In order to destroy all impurities of the creature, God sends this Wisdom to prepare you for divine union.

In order to be united to God, you must participate in His infinite stillness or you will prevent assimilation.

Therefore, your spirit can never arrive in divine union or become one with God until you have been reestablished in His rest and purity.

God purifies your spirit through Wisdom as refiners do metals in the furnace. Gold cannot be purified except by fire, which consumes all that is earthy and foreign.

The earthy part cannot be changed into gold. No, it must be melted and dissolved by force of the fire to separate every foreign particle. It must be cast again and again into the furnace until it has lost every trace of pollution and every possibility of being further purified.

Now, because of the perfect purity and simplicity of the gold, the goldsmith can no longer discover any adulterate mixture. The fire no longer touches it. If it were to remain in the furnace, its spotlessness would not be increased or its substance diminished.

The gold is now fit for the most exquisite workmanship. Hereafter, if the gold seems obscured or defiled, it is nothing more than accidental impurity occasioned by the contact from some foreign body, and it is only superficial. There is no hindrance to its service.

This superficial obscurity is widely different from its former debasement that was hidden in its nature.

Some superficial defects seem to be left by God in the greatest saints to keep them from pride, in order to preserve them from corruption, and to hide them in the secret of His presence.

However, I am not speaking of actual sin that separates us from perfect union; and I do not imagine it possible for anyone to draw such inferences from my simple illustration.

Furthermore, the pure and the impure gold are never mingled. The goldsmith cannot mix dross and gold.

What, then, will he do? He will purge out the dross with fire.

This is what Paul meant when he declared that *"the fire shall try every man's work of what sort it is"* (1 Corinthians 3:13). He added, *"If any man's work shall be burned, he shall suffer loss: but he himself shall be saved; yet so as by fire"* (verse 15).

Paul suggested that there are works so degraded by impure mixtures that, although the mercy of God accepts them, yet they must pass through the fire to be purged from self.

It is in this sense that God is said to examine and judge our righteousness. *"Therefore by the deeds of the law there shall no flesh be justified in his sight"* (Romans 3:20). God does this by His righteousness by faith in Jesus Christ.

Thus, divine justice and wisdom, like a pitiless and devouring fire, must destroy all that is earthly, fleshly, and carnal before the soul can be united to God.

This can never be accomplished by any works of the creature. In fact, the creature always submits with reluctance because he is so enamoured with self and so fearful of its destruction. If God did not act on him powerfully and with authority, he would never consent.

Yet I would add that, even though God does not rob man of his free will, man can always resist the divine operations. I would be in error to say God acts absolutely and without man's consent.

Let me, however, explain. By man giving God a passive consent, God may then assume full power and entire guidance. In the beginning of his conversion, man gave an unreserved surrender of himself to all that God wills. He thereby gave an active consent to whatever God might require.

But when God begins to purify, very often the soul does not perceive that these operations are intended for his good. Rather, he supposes the contrary.

When gold is first placed in the fire, it seems to blacken rather than brighten. The soul being purified senses this also, but he perceives that purity is lost.

If active and explicit consent was required, the soul could scarcely give it. No, in fact, he would often withhold it. All he does now is to remain firm in his passive consent, enduring as patiently as possible all these divine operations.

In this manner, God purifies a soul from its self-originated and multiplied operations that constitute a great dissimilitude between him and God.

This process of purifying may last a long time. But you must not become discouraged. Yield yourself to the divine Spirit until you are wholly absorbed in Him.

Twenty-two

Press On to Know God

But this one thing I do, forgetting those things which are behind, and reaching forth unto those things which are before, I press toward the mark for the prize of the high calling of God in Christ Jesus.
—*Philippians 3:13–14*

Wouldn't you say that a man had lost his senses, who, having begun a journey, would remain at his first place of lodging because he had been told that other travelers had enjoyed their stay there?

This is my prayer, then, for all who have read this little book. Press on toward the end. Don't stop at the first stage of your journey.

Don't think that there is no need for activity in the beginning of your travels to experience God. At first, it is your gate. When the Father calls you to fellowship with Him, you must heed the call to enter the narrow road.

The first helps you receive at the entrance of the road will, however, become detrimental to you as you progress in Jesus. Lay them aside. They will hinder you from reaching the end.

Follow the example of Paul, allowing yourself to be *"led by the Spirit of God"* (Romans 8:14). He will lead you to the ultimate goal of enjoying God forever.

While I am sure many of you will agree with me that enjoyment of God is the end for which alone we were created, I feel sure that many of you dread and even avoid the process.

How strange that many of you would entertain the thought that the cause of your trials brings evil and imperfection. Not so! That which is sent by God will only produce the perfection of His glory in your present and future existence.

Don't be ignorant of the fact that God is the Supreme Good. Essential blessedness consists in union with Him. Every saint will differ in glory according to the perfection of that union with Him.

Remember that you cannot generate enough activity to attain this union with God, since it is God Himself who must first draw us unto Himself. Then, in our simplicity and passivity, God will continue to unite us to Himself in a beautiful way.

The way is not dangerous. No, Jesus Christ has traveled on before us. This has enabled all to travel the road, to experience happiness, and to be called into fellowship with God, both in this life and the next.

I would emphasize my statement to you— you are called to enjoy God, not only His gifts to you.

While His gifts are beautiful, they cannot bring full contentment to your soul. The most exalted gifts from God cannot bring happiness unless the Giver also bestows Himself.

The whole desire of our heavenly Father is to give Himself to every creature according to the capacity in which we will receive Him.

Why, then, are you reluctant to be drawn to God? Why do you fear preparation for this divine union?

You will never be able to pretend you have reached this state if you have not. No one can. You will soon be found out, just as the person on the point of perishing from hunger cannot pretend to be full and satisfied. Some wish or word, some sigh or sign, will inevitably escape you, betraying the fact that you are far from satisfied.

You see, I have written all this to again say that you cannot attain this end by your own labor. I would not pretend to introduce any of you to it. I write only to point out the way that leads to finding God.

I beg you, do not become attached to the accommodations on the road or to any external practices that must all be left behind when God gives the signal to proceed.

Wouldn't it be a cruel injustice to lead a thirsty man to a cool spring, then bind him so he could not reach it, and watch him as he dies of thirst? Yet this is what we do every day.

Our journey to God has its beginning, its progress, and its termination. The nearer we come to the end of the road, the further away is its beginning. We must leave one to arrive at another.

Press on, press on, press on to know God!

Do not be like the majority of mankind who pride themselves on their own blind wisdom.

Oh, what truth Jesus revealed when He said, *"I thank thee, O Father, Lord of heaven and earth, because thou hast hid these things from the wise and prudent, and hast revealed them unto babes"* (Matthew 11:25).